Sacred

Photographs by Lisa Dunlap

Poems by Linda Hasley

Sacred

Photographs by Lisa Dunlap

Poems by Linda Hasley

Printed in Canada by Friesens Corporation
Book production by Jim Jakubowski, Greg Dunn
and Karen McDiarmid

Twin Spirit Creations
P. O. Box 918
Royal Oak, MI 48068-0918
http://www.sacredportraitsphotography.com

ISBN # 0-9766497-8-0

Authors' Notes

Writing poetry has been a love of mine for many years. I started writing while in college and wrote passionately about the reality of my childhood. I discovered that I was able to heal a lot of my unresolved pain through the written word. From that point on, I knew that I had to keep writing the absolute truth in all its rawness and beauty.

After the birth of my first child, I struggled with many new emotions. Along with the intense love for my baby, I also felt a great deal of anguish. I turned to my poetry to help transcend the anger, pain and frustration of this cell-changing transition into motherhood. This process was very cathartic and helped me to see the beauty in my day-to-day life as my family expanded. I believe my poetry reflects the unspoken truths about motherhood and shows that it is normal to experience both the glory and the heartache of family life. I know that Spirit has guided my writing every step of the way, and for that, I am truly grateful. This book is an offering to those who are seeking sanity where there are myths, and is meant to provide hope to other mothers so they, too, can live more fully in love. ~ Linda

Being in nature with my camera has always been a meditation for me — a way to connect myself with a higher source. As I looked through my camera lens at a beautiful landscape, I was able to see God's glory looking back at me. Over time, I realized that my mission was to see and record the divine beauty of this world as if through God's eye.

Then my nieces and nephews began arriving into this world. As I focused my camera on them, and then on my pregnant sisters, friends and, eventually, my clients, that precious connection to Spirit came through once again. To me, there is nothing more awe-inspiring and sacred than beholding the miracle of life: a pregnant woman, a newborn baby, a father gently holding his child. I am blessed to be allowed to witness and capture this through the lens of my camera. This book honors the sacredness of the soul and the connection to God that we all possess. It is my great joy to share this time with the families that I photograph. I am grateful for their trust and inspired by the love these parents have for their children. ~ Lisa

Dedications

This book is dedicated to the families who grace these pages. I am honored to have shared a moment with you on your sacred journey. Thank you for your trust and enthusiasm. Without you, this book would not have been possible. ~ Lisa

To my lovely family: Dan, Libby, Anna and Grace. The life we share makes my heart sing. I am truly blessed. Thank you for the everyday richness that inspires me to write. ~ Linda

Acknowledgments

To Spirit, our souls have deepened as we have opened to your divine guidance. Your presence in the pages of this book is undeniable. Our gratitude is endless.

To our publishers group, thank you for your unwavering commitment to the highest integrity and truth. To walk this earth in light with you, our fellow travelers, is a gift.

A gracious thank-you to Jim Jakubowski, whose excellent computer skills helped bring this book to life. Your deep respect in honoring its sacredness was invaluable.

To Greg Dunn and Karen McDiarmid, thank you for being part of this book's beautiful journey.

To our dear families and community of friends, you grace our lives with your sweet love, enthusiasm and generous support. ~ Namaste

Introduction

To read the heartfelt, passionate words of a mother in search of the truth, no matter how raw, no matter how painful it may be. To gaze at the pure essence of mothers and fathers and children in photographs taken by a woman who uses her camera lens to capture images, as if through the eye of God. To see the visions of two vibrant souls come together in a creation of beauty and of truth and of love, deeply inspired me. It was as though the intrinsic weave of sacred words and images invited me to bring my God-self forward. Thus, "The Gift" was born.

~ Lauren Dembs Lesson ~ author, mother of three

The Gift

The gift you have given to me is remembrance.
Remembrance of sacredness, of what is holy,
of what lies beyond beauty, of illuminated love,
of God, of a place where there are no words.
Where eyes meet eyes with an absolute knowing
of what is being expressed.
Of souls dancing on clouds, of all that is bliss,
of passion, of what flows,
of essence, of what truly is.
The gift that I will give to you
is to allow your gift to penetrate every cell of my being,
to let its energy spiral in and generate the growth
that my highest self so deeply desires.
The gift that I give to you is to let your vision
touch my vision,
to let your truth, your light,
your beauty, your essence
touch mine.
So that I, too, will fly.

~ Lauren Dembs Lesson © 2005

~It is not a slight thing when they, who are so fresh from God, love us~

Charles Dickens

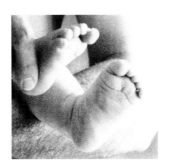

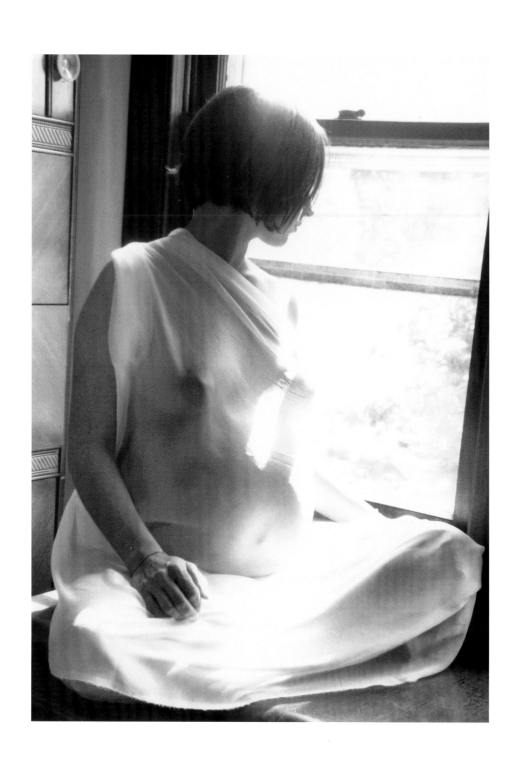

Goddess Within

I close my eyes
to catch a glimpse
of the goddess within.

She's never far
always near,
just under my skin.

She takes many forms
to keep me strong,
Goddess of Motherhood
Poetry and Song.

She whispers softly in my ears,
helping me conquer
all of my fears.

But sweet goddess,
I must know,
why your face
you do not show.

I wonder, could it be
that I am you
and you are me?

A Mere Woman

One more push
and your red wrinkled body
slips into this world.
Thick dark hair, matted and wet.
Arms and legs flailing.
Your soft, gurgled cries fill up the room
as they hand you to me.
Holding you close, I stare at your
sweet, round face
and wonder why
you chose me.

Me,
a mere woman,
still battling the demons
of a crushed childhood.
Me,
a mere woman,
still struggling to embrace
her femininity.
Me,
a mere woman,
still fighting for the right
to live in joy.

Our eyes meet
as I pull you to my breast.
Who is this soul,
this beautiful soul
who still chose me?

A mere woman.

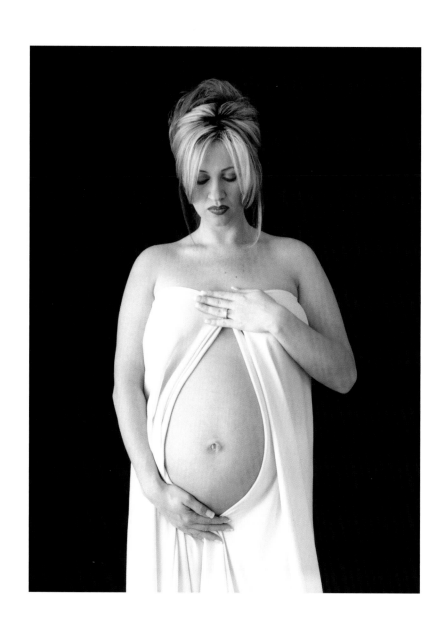

For Anna

There's a spot
tucked in sweetly
just behind your knee
where a tiny pair of
upraised wings adorns your body.
Creamy-white in color
you trace them with your fingers
and marvel at their exactness.

Those wings,
a precious gift from God
just before your birth.
A souvenir to help remind you
of where you came from.

On some days,
if I watch closely enough,
I can almost see your wings
as they unfurl
in all their glory.
Flexing and stretching,
ready for flight as you
gallop across the lawn.
Your soul longing to soar
to a place not of this earth.
To a place where
light touches only light,
where once again
your spirit can fly free.

Nightcap

You and I lie
face-to-face
on a white shag rug.
Your fuzzy little head
rests sleepily on my shoulder,
your arms and legs
curled tight against my body.
The night air settles
quietly between us
as I pull you closer.

Humming softly,
I breathe you in.
Warm, fragrant air
saturating my lungs.
With eyes closed,
I inhale deeper
as your sweet
intoxicating scent
slowly fills
the empty spaces
of my soul.

The Family Bed

In the quiet moments before dawn,
silver light softens
the dark corners of our bedroom.

Under rumpled covers, we lie together:
mother,
father,
daughter,
daughter.

Skin touching skin,
warm and moist.
Arms and legs intertwined
like a finely woven blanket.

In unison,
lungs fill and release
the cool morning air
as we begin our day together,
our journey together.

Mother,
father,
daughter,
daughter.

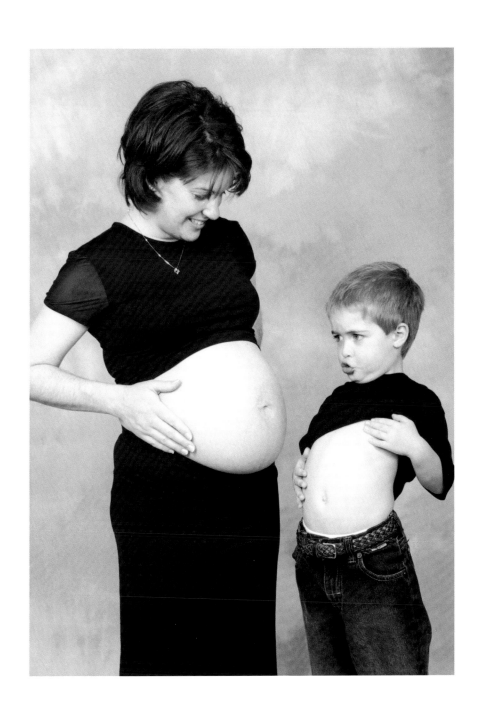

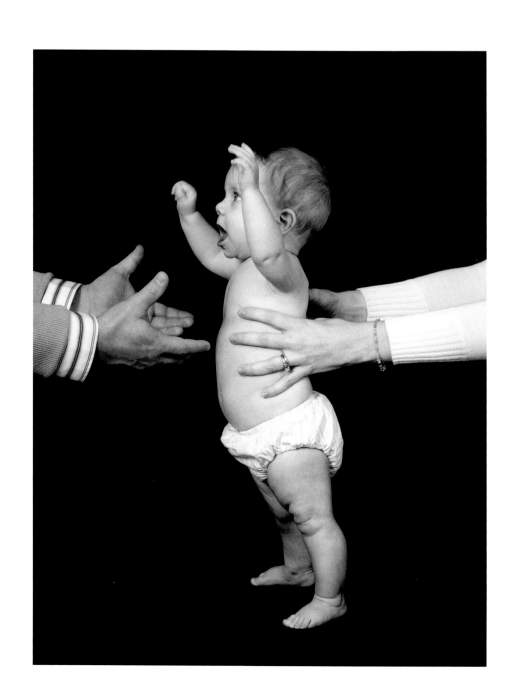

The Afterbirth

I stand naked
in the shower,
hot water
pounding
my bloated form.

One hand
shielding breasts
too swollen
with milk,
the other steadying
shaky limbs
against cold tile.

With head throbbing,
the sound starts
low in my belly
and gradually moves
upward.
My stomach tightens
as it reaches my throat,
and I begin to wail.
Slowly, softly
my voice begins to rise
as gushing water
mercilessly
strips away
every last cell
of my former self.

Two Souls

Two souls nestle deep
within the womb,
one head pressing against
the small of the other's back.
Tiny knees and feet
tucked tight
in the fetal position.

Newly formed limbs
jerk and stretch
as they reach toward
one another,
and gently push
each other away.

Two hearts beat
in true cadence,
the rhythm strong and steady,
beating as one.

Two souls inhale
liquid life together.
Fragile lungs breathe in
and then out — practicing.
Practicing for the divine moment
when the call of the birth song
brings forth life,
brings forth separation,
brings forth an end to this
perfect, symbiotic world.

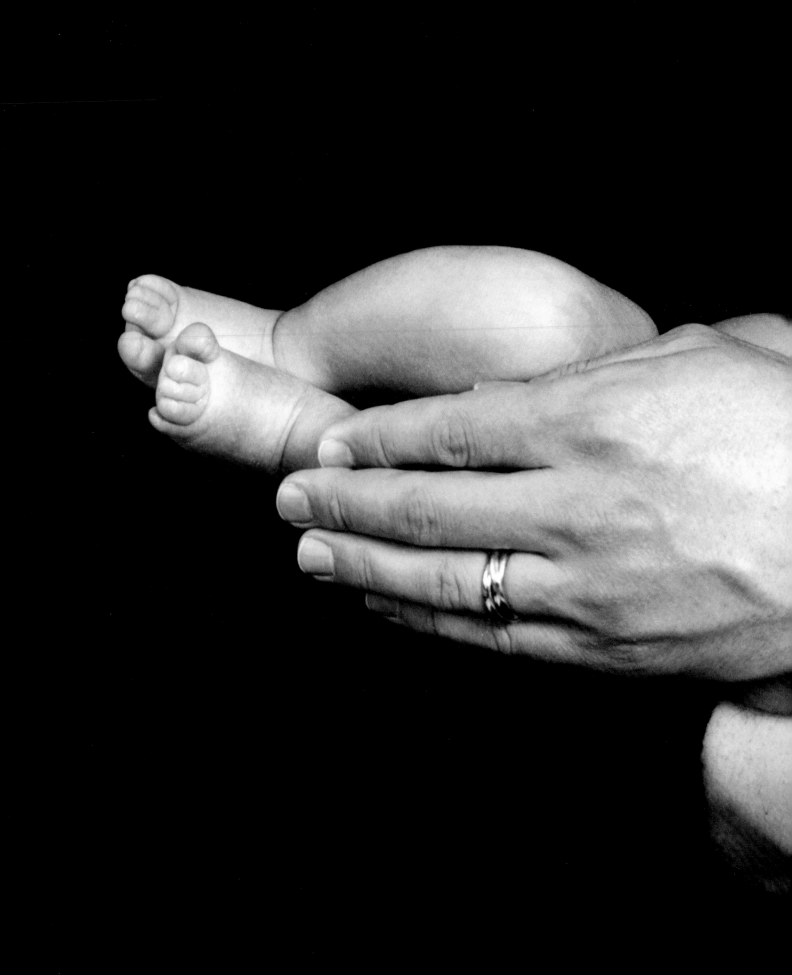

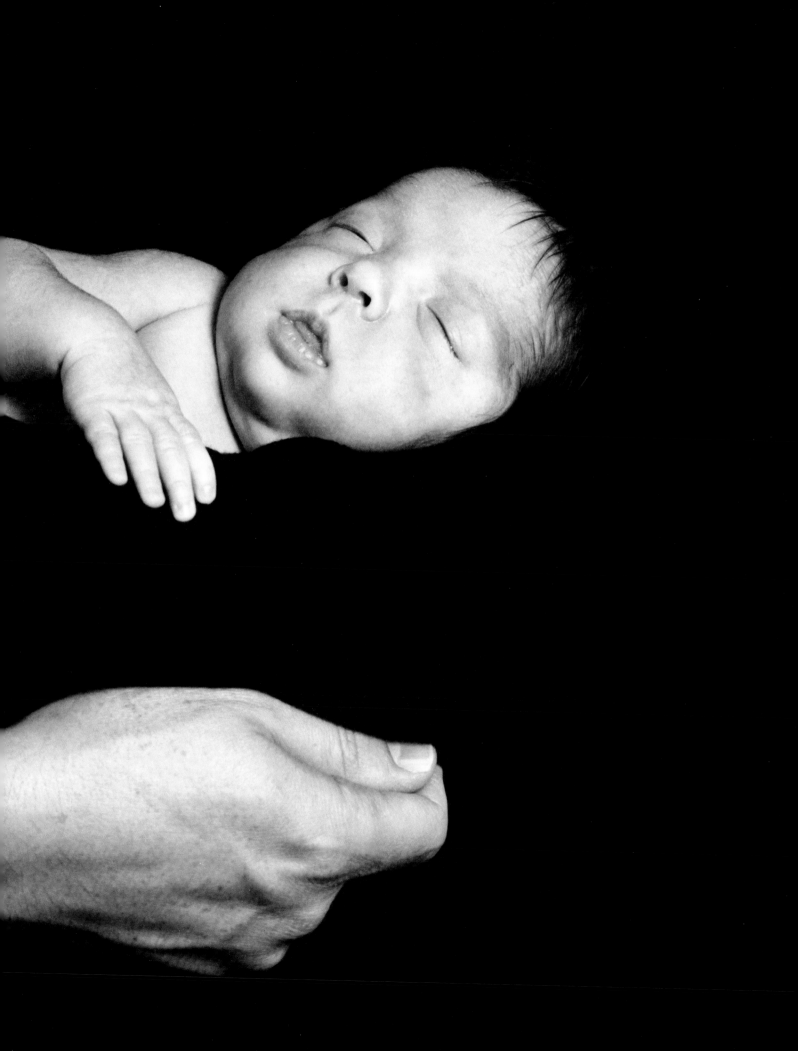

A Circle of Women

A circle of women unite
who believe it is better
to speak truth
than it is to deceive.

We are women of integrity,
beauty and soul.
Raising our children
in consciousness
is truly our goal.

We draw on each other's
wisdom and strength,
and strive to be
present, at any length.

We share our frustrations,
joys and victories,
hoping to impact
our children's destinies.

Our teachers have arrived —
they are the youth.
With voices strong,
let us spread our truth.

A Father's Voyage

I sit next to you
on this two-person sailboat
as we glide across
liquid silver.
August wind at our backs,
the sail white, full.

You begin to tell me
of summers past,
of the hours you spent
sailing these fragrant waters.

I can almost
picture you then,
teenage boy with
sun-streaked hair,
skin golden brown.
Blue eyes squinting as
you carefully study the
intimate relationship
between wind and sail.

I wonder if you knew then
what a beautiful soul
you had within you or
that your strength and spirit
would someday be needed
to gently guide
three lovely daughters
through turbulent waters.

The breeze begins to fade now
as the sun slowly
descends in the west.
Pulling in the sail,
you steer the boat
gradually up into the wind
and point us toward home.

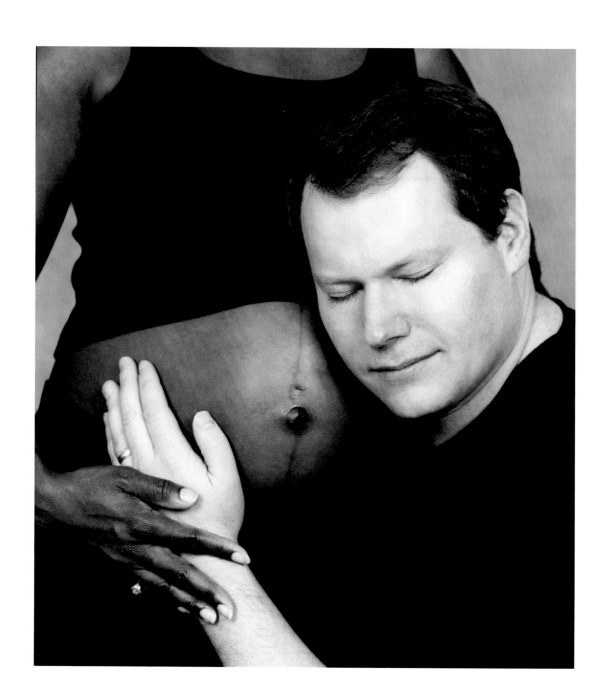

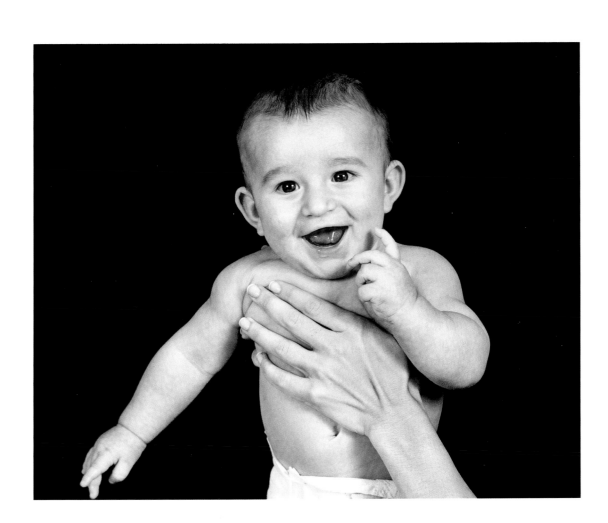

To Be Three ~ I watch you from across the table. Your head down, golden hair spilling across your brow. Chirping a sweet singsong your tiny fingers grasp plastic scissors as you slowly move the blunted blade through orange, purple and green paper. Your brown eyes gleam as carefully cut treasures fall to the table and lightly float to the floor.

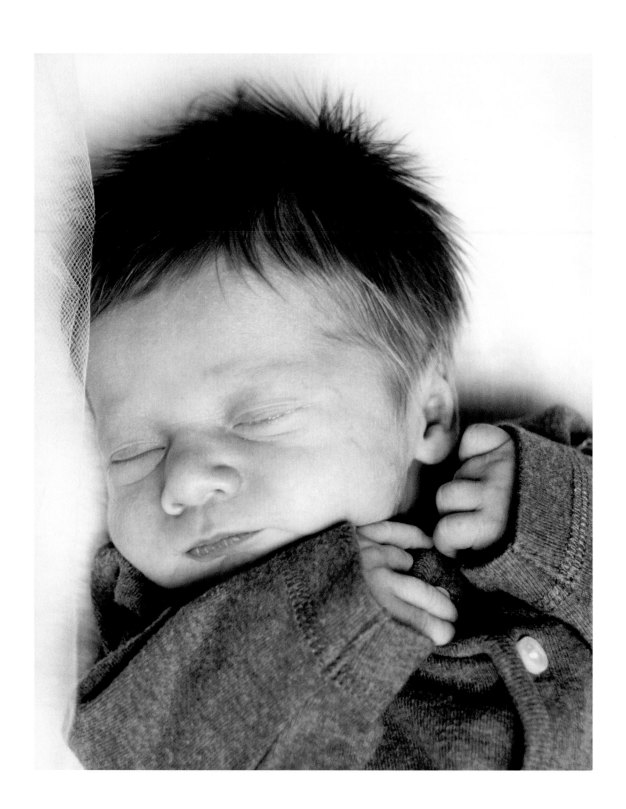

Night Rhythms

Your razor-sharp screams
slice open the black night.
With knees drawn up
tight against my chest,
I burrow my head deeper
under my pillow
and silently pray for sleep.

One more explosion
and I throw myself
over the side of the bed
and stagger down the stairs.
I find you at the edge
of your crib,
skinny little limbs
reaching out for me.
I quickly pull you
into my arms,
your body hot with fever.
I stumble into the rocking chair,
and we begin.
Moving quietly, methodically
back and forth,
back and forth.
My mind drifts,
aching toward numbness
as my heart slows
to the rhythm of
this life called motherhood.

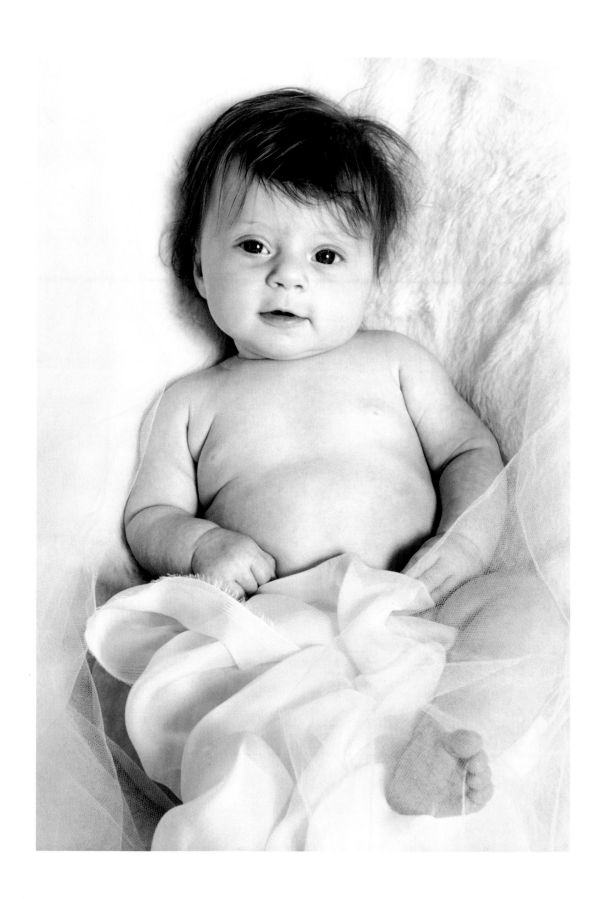

For the Love of Bugs

I watch from the kitchen window
as morning sun stretches
toward noon.
I see three little girls
on hands and knees with
hair dangling down —
one blond head,
two brown.

I watch as eager little fingers
carefully pull back
mossy garden rocks,
searching for crawling treasures.
The youngest one holds up
a small pill bug that has rolled
itself into a tiny black ball.
With squeals of delight,
her older sisters huddle in
tightly to get a closer look.
My heart sings as, one by one,
they softly kiss the roly-poly bug and
return it safely to its home.

Dreaming of Grace

You spoke to me in a dream
right after the birth
of our second daughter.
My womb still
ripe, warm.
You told me your name
and showed me your
lovely, round face
for only an instant,
and told me
you wanted to come
and be our third daughter.

Even when you were
sick inside me,
the doctors in their white coats
guessing at your fate,
I held onto that dream,
to that sweet vision
of your face.

I hold you now,
fresh from God.
Heartbeat strong,
mouth roving.
Breathing deeply,
I pull you close
as our eyes meet
for a second time.

Libby's Temple

Pulling back
the shower curtain,
I find you standing there.
Damp mist swirling
around your almost
3-year-old frame.

As I step gingerly
onto the bathroom rug,
your tiny hands
reach for my tummy.
Little fingers lightly trace
purple and white stretch marks
etched in loose skin.

Singing sweetly,
you gently place
tender lips on
my soft, wet belly
and kiss the place
where you once lived.
Your home.
Your temple.
A place where we
were once one.

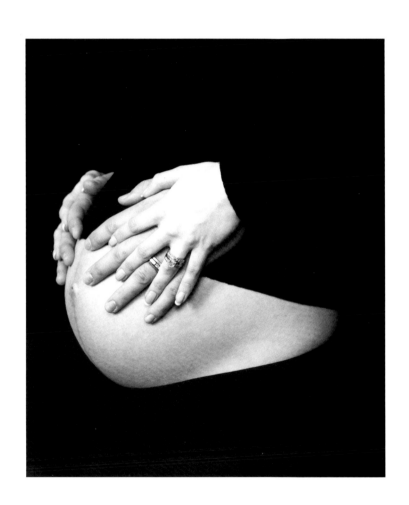

Grateful

Still in my pajamas,
I sit cross-legged
on my bedroom floor.
Mountains of dirty laundry
surround me.
Dingy whites, darks and reds
piled high in all directions.

With a heavy sigh,
I toss week-old underwear
onto the piles and wonder
if this day will ever end.
Then I hear it,
very faint at first.
Like birds chirping
or dogs barking in the distance.
As the sound gets louder,
I realize it is laughter.
Sweet, wonderful girl laughter
bubbling up through the floorboards.

The laughter begins
to flood the room
as my three daughters
bound up the stairs.
They greet me with
hugs and wet kisses
as we fall together
in a giggly heap.
My spirit lifts
as hot, glorious tears
stream down my cheeks.